# of Being
# an Altar Server

Father Joseph Champlin

**Resurrection Press**
An Imprint of
**CATHOLIC BOOK PUBLISHING CORP.**
Totowa • New Jersey

Imprimatur: ✠ Most Reverend Thomas J. Costello, D.D.
        *Vicar General, Diocese of Syracuse, New York*

Scripture quotations are from the New Revised Standard Version of the Bible, copyright 1989 by the Division of Christian Education of the National Council of the Churches of Christ in the USA. Used by permission. All rights reserved.

First published in March, 2002 by Resurrection Press, Catholic Book Publishing Corporation.

Copyright © 2002 by Rev. Joseph Champlin

ISBN 1-878718-66-5

Library of Congress Catalog Number: 2001-132738

Cover design by John Murello

Photos by Edward J. Long © 2002. All rights reserved.

Printed in Canada.

3  4  5  6  7  8  9

Pope John Paul II spoke to a gathering of 2,000 young men and women altar servers gathered in Rome on August 12, 2001.

Our Holy Father, among other remarks to them, said:

*The altar server occupies a privileged place in the liturgical celebration. The altar server presents himself to a community and experiences firsthand that Jesus Christ is present and active in every liturgical act. Jesus is present when the community comes together to pray and render praise to God. Jesus is present in the Word of sacred Scripture. Jesus is present above all in the Eucharist under the signs of bread and wine. He acts through the priest who, in the person of Christ, celebrates the holy Mass and administers the sacraments.*

*Therefore, in the liturgy, you are much more than simple "helpers of the parish priest." Above all, you are servers of Jesus Christ, of the eternal High Priest. Thus, you, altar servers, are called in particular to be young friends of Jesus. Be determined to go deeper and to cultivate this friendship with him. You will discover that in Jesus you have found a true friend for life.*

# Table of Contents

# Introduction

FOR some youngsters at the Cathedral of the Immaculate Conception in Syracuse, New York, fourth grade becomes a turning point in their lives. It is at this age that boys and girls may become altar servers in our hundred-year-old, large and beautiful church.

Fifth grader Robert trained during the winter and served for the first time at a 9:30 a.m. Sunday Mass.

He was quite nervous beforehand, but no more so than his parents as they awaited their son's appearance at the altar in a white server's robe. Afterwards Robert wore a huge smile on his face and his parents proudly embraced him.

Several weeks later, Robert wrote down why he liked being a server:

*Here are three reasons why I like being an altar server. One is because I know I am serving God and his message. Another is because I like it and have fun doing it. Last it makes me feel good about myself. All in all I am really glad I am an altar server.*

Robert also enjoys drawing and made this sketch of his altar-serving experience.

Tall and thin, Laura is a junior in high school, an honor student who both marches in the color guard of her school's world-class marching band and performs in several of the school's musical productions. She also works part time as receptionist in our parish office and as weekend sacristan in the church itself. In addition, Laura has been my main guide and helper in preparing this book.

She writes about her own joy in being a server:

*Altar serving has made a lasting impact on my life and it is something that I will take with me and value throughout my adulthood.*

*I know that being behind the scenes and helping to run the Mass has taught me to become a part of the ceremony in my heart and my mind, rather than just being a spectator. Serving has especially been important to me as a female because it is probably the closest opportunity that women have to interact with the all-male leaders of our faith.*

*Knowing the meaning behind the Mass has helped me form a strong bond with God and a love for worshiping Him. I always thought that eventually young altar servers would grow up and lose interest in serving, but every year I enjoy this blessed duty more and more.*

*I have learned new things about myself and my relationship with God that have helped shape who I am in our Christian community.*

Some former servers begin again at an older age to assist around the altar during our daily noon Mass.

Robert, 53 and father of three, is one of them. A graduate of Central Michigan College, he now works for the county as an economic developer.

Quite often he walks a block or two from his office to the Cathedral and serves at this mid-day Mass.

His words about the joy of serving thus cover almost a half-century of living on this earth:

> *Our faith teaches us that the Mass is the celebration of the Eucharist. This is where our loving Savior becomes present at the altar just as he was at the Last Supper. This is done through the priest as the celebrant. The primary duty of the altar server is to assist the priest.*
>
> *I was an altar server from the time I was in third grade until I graduated from high school. Actually, my initial interest was to be a choirboy. However, God did not give me that particular talent and the good sister in charge said that I should stick to being an altar server. It was quite interesting being an altar server in the 50s and 60s. I witnessed the Mass going from Latin to English, the altar turning around with the priest facing the people and the increased participation of the congregation.*
>
> *All three of my children were altar servers. In fact, my youngest son complained of having to serve after Confirmation. It was no longer*

*the cool thing to do. I explained to him that I was still an altar server at the Cathedral. I asked him to think of what happens on that altar. Furthermore, I explained what an awesome responsibility and honor it is to be a small part of that celebration and how I feel just a little bit closer to God by being a server. How can we not serve when we think of what Jesus did for us?*

We will hear from others in this book: boys and girls like fourth grader Robert, teenagers like Laura, and adults like 53-year-old Robert.

Good servers understand what the Mass is about (serving with my head), know what needs to be done (serving with my hands), and carry out their duties with a proper attitude (serving with my heart). I hope and pray that this little book will help both young and older persons become better servers and also experience the joy of being a server.

# — Part One —

# Serving with My Head

**Lauren, Fourth Grade**

I like being an altar server because it makes me feel like I am in God's arms and I feel blessed. I also love doing it because it's fun. I can pray and do everything the priest tells me.

Altar serving is part of life to me. It makes me feel happy. I like doing it because I help the priest. I remember what he needs and I and the other server or servers bring what he needs to him.

Altar serving is very cool. I also like to do it because I am not worried anymore. I do it because God is happy when I do it. I am not worried any more because I know what to do now. I am happy I am an altar server. I am very happy to serve God.

# ~ 1 ~

# The Overall Plan of the Mass

**Megan, First Year High School**

*When I was first asked to become an altar server, I was quite nervous. But over the past few years, being an altar server has become a privilege. When I am standing up there, on the altar, with a congregation looking at me, I not only feel like a role-model for the younger kids, but I also feel as if I am giving something back to the Church. Altar serving keeps you interested in the Mass, and makes you feel as if you have a special part in the Mass. Altar serving can also make you feel especially helpful when a certain priest gets a nosebleed at the chair and forgets or does not know to squeeze his nose to stop it.*

✝

The way we celebrate Mass today is not exactly the way it was celebrated two thousand years ago.

## Beginnings

The beginning took place on a Thursday night in an upper room with Jesus and his twelve closest friends, the Apostles. We read a description of that first Mass in the Gospels of Matthew, Mark and Luke and in the First Letter of St. Paul to the Corinthians (Matthew 26:26-30; Mark 14:22-26; Luke 22:14-20; 1 Corinthians 11:17-34).

Jesus gathered them together for a special religious meal. They listened to a few passages from the holy Bible and sang some spiritual hymns. Then Christ took bread and wine (probably mixed with a little water), gave thanks and said: "This is my body," "This is my blood." After those words, he passed the blessed food and drink around to each person saying: "Take and eat," Take and drink."

The Greek word for "giving thanks" is *eucharist* and that is why we often call our Mass the Eucharist or a Eucharistic Celebration.

At the end of this sacred meal, called the Last Supper, Jesus commanded his apostles and those who succeeded them to "Do this in memory of me."

## Additions and Changes

After Christ rose from the dead, his followers celebrated the Eucharist as he directed. But over these twenty centuries, church leaders have surrounded what Jesus did with many prayers, special clothes or vestments for the priest, and different actions. What Christ did remains the same, but the additions keep changing.

For example, less than fifty years ago, priests generally offered Mass in Latin, with their back to the people in the pews, who, for the most part, watched this holy event in silence. Today, as we know, priests usually face the congregation and celebrate in the people's language while those in the pews or seats actively participate.

Those changes help make what Jesus did clearer to the people and give them a richer share in what the Mass offers them. We can expect such changes to continue as the world around us changes.

## Like a Diamond

We might compare the Mass to a diamond ring. The core or the essential part of the ring is the precious diamond. But the diamond rests in a special setting and is attached to a circular band. Over the years the band often wears thin and the setting loses some of its beauty. Both need to be repaired or replaced. But the diamond remains.

So, too, with the Mass or the Eucharist. The bread, water and wine, the words of Jesus, and Communion always must be there. But the prayers, vestments, and actions have, can, and should change with the passage of time. Otherwise, they will take away from the Mass's beauty instead of enhancing it.

## The Mass Today

The form of the Mass we follow today dates back to 1970. It contains four parts:

*Introductory Rites:* This relatively brief part includes the entrance procession, sign of the cross and greeting, a penitential rite, the Gloria of praise during most of the year, and the opening prayer.

*Liturgy of the Word:* Our attention for this part shifts to the *ambo,* pulpit or lectern and centers around readings from the Bible followed by the homily or sermon, the Creed, and the General Intercessions or Prayers of the Faithful.

*Liturgy of the Eucharist:* We move for this part over to the altar for the Preparation of the Gifts, the Eucharistic Prayer, and Communion.

*Concluding Rites:* We return to the presiding priest's chair for this final, very brief part which contains announcements, a blessing, and a dismissal or sending forth.

## Two Mountains

We might simply diagram the Mass as a movement with two mountains, one slightly larger than the other, each with an upward and a downward slope.

After gathering, we first speak to God and then God speaks to us; next we give to God and God gives to us. The first mountain occurs around the ambo; the second around the altar. The priest or deacon then sends us out into the world.

- We gather and prepare our hearts.

- First Mountain

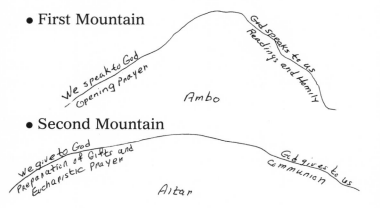

- Second Mountain

• Having received God's guidance through the sacred words and received God's strength through Christ's Body and Blood, we go forth to bring the Good News to others.

## Names to Know

*Presiding Priest or Celebrant:* This is the priest who offers the Mass. The most common title is "Presiding Priest," since he presides over the gathered people, the Liturgy of the Word, the Liturgy of the Eucharist, and the dismissal rite. Formerly, he was often called the Celebrant. However, today we better understand that all present celebrate the Eucharist.

*Concelebrant(s):* When another priest joins the presiding priest for Mass, he is called a concelebrant. He sits and stands by the presiding priest and shares some of the eucharistic prayer with him.

*Usher:* Ushers seek to maintain peaceful order in the church during Mass. They sometimes also act as greeters or hospitality ministers. They seat those arriving for worship. They gather the collection of offerings and arrange for them to be brought forward to the altar. They stand prepared to resolve any emergencies which may occur.

~ 2 ~

# The Vestments for Mass

Matthew and Andrea, Twins, also First Year High
School Students.

**Andrea**

*Being a server makes me feel special,
because I know that I'm not only helping the
priest during Mass, but I'm also serving God.
When I'm serving with beginner servers, I
feel like a leader. Ever since I started being
an altar server, I've paid more attention to
the Mass. Therefore, the meaning is clearer
to me. Being an altar server not only makes
me feel closer to God, but also to my parish
community. Being a server is a privilege and
it'll stick with me for the rest of my life!*

**Matthew**

*Being an altar server is great. I learn and
understand the meaning much better. I now
know all the prayers and everything that*

*goes on during the Mass. The Mass is much more enjoyable when you are a participant in it. The Mass used to seem boring when I wasn't an altar server, but now it is not boring at all. I am very happy that I got a chance to be an altar server and that I became one. It has changed my life forever!*

✠

For the first few centuries, the priest celebrating Mass usually wore the ordinary clothes of the time. Gradually there was a shift in the way people dressed for everyday activities.

However, to set off the sacred action of the Mass from other activities, the Church retained for the priest those garments worn as ordinary clothing in earlier days. But it gradually made adjustments in them and, much later, tended to add a spiritual meaning to each article.

## Altar Server Garments

Altar servers usually wear vestments especially designed for them. They, too, have a spiritual meaning. Pope John Paul II spoke not long ago to several thousand young men and women altar servers. Among his remarks, he said:

"The altar server's clothing is very special. It recalls the garment that each one puts on when he is welcomed in Jesus Christ in the community. I am referring to the baptismal gown, whose profound meaning St. Paul clarifies: 'For all of you who were baptized into Christ have clothed yourselves with Christ' (Galatians 3:27).

"Even if you, dear altar servers, can no longer fit into your baptismal gown, you have put on (the clothing) of altar servers. Yes, baptism is the point of departure of your 'authentic liturgical service' which places you next to your bishops, priests, and deacons."

## Mass Vestments

Here, with a little explanation, are the vestments which a priest wears for the Mass or Eucharist. As the author of this book, I get to model them for you.

**Amice**

In early days, people wore a kind of scarf around their neck for warmth. It also protected the outer garment from being soiled by perspiration. For various reasons, today the amice is no longer essential and not all priests wear it at Mass. Since sometimes it was used almost as a hood, the Church connected the amice with a passage from the Bible which speaks about a helmet of salvation. Thus, the amice was to remind us that God and God's grace protect us from evil.

## Alb

For everyday use, first century people wore this long, flowing inner garment. The Church added to its practical value the symbolic meaning of purity.

## Cincture

Climbing up or down stairs or just moving around wearing the lengthy alb could be difficult. This cord, rope or belt, tied in a special way, enables a priest or deacon to adjust the alb to a proper length.

The Church applies to the cincture the biblical passage about girding or preparing ourselves for spiritual battles.

## Stole

The stole symbolizes that one has been ordained or received the sacrament of Holy Orders: a deacon, priest, or bishop. The deacon's stole is worn across his chest from the shoulder to the side; the priest's stole hangs around the neck and falls straight down the front. Deacons, priests, or bishops wear a stole whenever they carry out their task as an ordained person—for example, baptizing, anointing the sick, or confirming. It is a symbol of their offices and the authority which accompanies those offices.

**Chasuble**

The outer garment worn in early days we call the chasuble or "little house." In its original ordinary use, the chasuble provided warmth for the wearer and protection from the elements like rain or snow. Today it is an outer vestment for the priest. The basic color of the chasuble reflects the season or the feast. Moreover, often religious symbols are added to this vestment, like a cross, wheat, or grapes.

**Year of Grace**

Year after year the Church inspires us with a series of annual celebrations. One honors saints; the other honors Jesus.

Those honoring saints have a fixed date in the calendar.

For example, the feast of Saint Paul Miki and his companions who were martyrs in Japan, put to death because of their Christian faith, falls on February 6. For St. Patrick of Ireland the celebration occurs on March 17 and St. Joseph on March 19. We celebrate the feast of Mary's Assumption on August 15 and her Immaculate Conception on December 8.

When these fall on a Sunday, which is always a more important feast day, the saint's celebration is not observed that year or is shifted to another day.

Those celebrations honoring Jesus cover the entire year and their date of celebration varies.

• We prepare for Christ's coming during the four weeks of Advent.

• We celebrate his birth and early life for several weeks after Christmas.

• We reflect upon and rejoice over his good news for us during the month or so between the end of the Christmas season and the beginning of Lent.

• We prepare for the sacred events of Holy Week and the joys of Easter for forty days or some six weeks of the Lenten season.

• We celebrate his rising from the dead and unique presence in our midst for fifty days until Pentecost.

• We relive the Coming of the Holy Spirit upon Mary, the Apostles and other followers of Christ on Pentecost Sunday.

• We resume our reflection and rejoicing over his good news for us during the months of what is called Ordinary time from June through November.

**Vestment Colors**

The color of the chasuble and other items in the sanctuary change for each of these seasons and /or feasts. Each color has a special meaning.

Purple indicates a time of expectation, purification or penance. White or gold expresses joy and triumph. Red is a sign of royalty, fire, and martyrdom. Green symbolizes life and growth.

The following simplified table of highlights of the Church Year may help clarify the meaning of the colors and the Church Year.

| Season or Feast | Time & Meaning | Liturgical Color |
|---|---|---|
| Advent | Four weeks of preparation for Christ's coming on December 25 | Purple |
| Christmas-Epiphany | Christ's birth and early manifestation | White |
| Lent | 40 days of penitential preparation for baptism and Easter | Purple |
| Easter | Christ's Resurrection and the Risen Lord's appearance to his followers | White |
| Pentecost | Descent of the Holy Spirit (Acts 2) | Red |
| Ordinary Time | The Church hearing and living Jesus' message | Green |

You may now understand a bit better the overall plan of the Mass and the vestments worn at the Eucharist. In the next chapter we will examine the various materials used during Eucharistic celebrations.

## Names to Know

*Special (extraordinary) Ministers of the Eucharist:* These are lay servers, men and women, who are specially trained and designated to assist with the distribution of Holy Communion. This may include taking the Eucharist to those confined at home or in a hospital and unable to attend Mass. They may also preside at a Communion service when the priest is not available.

*Lector and reader:* These persons proclaim the biblical readings and the prayer of the faithful or general intercessions. The Church encourages us at each Mass to have as many readers as readings (one or two), but sometimes only a single person is on hand for the task.

*Cantor:* Congregational singing is an essential part of today's Mass. A cantor or leader of song helps the community achieve that goal in various ways, often by chanting verses of a psalm while the people respond with a common antiphon or short musical phrase.

## ~ 3 ~

# The Materials for Mass

**Rachel, Seventh Grade**

*Every Sunday when I come to church, I hope to have the chance to be honored with the opportunity to serve on God's altar. It is a privilege that I enjoy very much. I feel like I am part of the Mass, and this has helped me to interpret every Sunday much more clearly than before I was a server. I get to help the priest not only do his job, but proclaim it to others as well. Being an altar server means so much to me. I am grateful for this opportunity of a lifetime.*

A central feature of any Catholic church is the *crucifix,* a cross with an image of Jesus attached to it. It may be large and fixed to a wall or smaller and near the altar. It also could be part of the processional cross carried to and from the sanctuary before and after Mass.

The *sanctuary* is the elevated space which contains the altar, the ambo (lectern or pulpit), and presiding priest's chair.

*Candles* are an important part of Catholic Christian worship. Jesus said that he was the light of the world, a light shining in darkness. The burning candles which surround the altar remind us that Christ our light is present in a unique way during Mass.

The *tabernacle,* with a lamp or candle constantly burning beside or above it, holds containers of consecrated or blessed small pieces of bread (called hosts) which were transformed during the Mass into the Body of Christ. The burning lamp or candle reminds us that Jesus the Lord is truly present within the tabernacle. Because of our belief that God is present in that space, we make a reverence toward it (a bow or genuflection) whenever passing in front of the tabernacle.

We use *incense* at Mass on special solemn occasions and especially at funerals. There are two items needed for this: First, a vessel, sometimes called the *thurible* or censer, which contains the burning charcoal; second, a small cup, sometimes called the *boat,* containing the incense itself (see page 55).

The burning incense symbolizes our prayer rising to God. It also is a sign of respect and honor for the person or object being incensed.

In today's Eucharists there are two essential Mass books; generally they are large, and often red

in color. One is the *Sacramentary* with over two thousand prayers, several of which are chosen for each Mass and proclaimed from either the chair or altar. The second is the *Lectionary* of biblical readings which are proclaimed from the ambo.

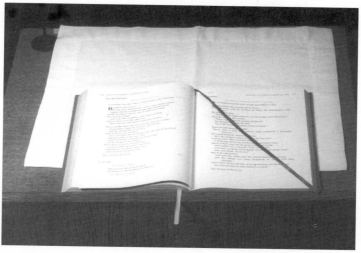

Most churches also have a *Book of the Gospels* which is held high during the entrance procession and placed on the altar. Later the priest or deacon carries it solemnly to the ambo and proclaims the gospel assigned to that day from it. These readings have been taken from the Lectionary and are reprinted in this richly decorated Book of the Gospels.

A white cloth covers the top of the altar. At the preparation of the gifts, servers bring to the altar a smaller white linen cloth called the *corporal.* Corporal comes from the Latin word meaning body. It is thus a suitable name for this cloth upon which the Body of Christ will later rest. The corporal traditionally has a small red cross woven into it and folds in a way that nine squares are formed in the cloth.

Another white linen cloth with a red cross woven into it, but rectangular in shape, is called the *purificator.* The priest, deacon or eucharistic minister employs a purificator to purify the chalice and other cups used for the distribution of the Precious Blood in Communion. The server places a purificator at the right of the corporal during the preparation of gifts; others bring additional purificators to the altar at Communion time.

The *chalice* will contain the wine to become the Precious Blood of Christ. It must be made of noble metal or other solid materials which do not absorb the wine or Precious Blood. Those distributing Communion use the chalice and smaller cups for that purpose.

The *paten* or plate holds the large and small hosts or wafers to be consecrated by the priest at Mass. Patens are made of noble metal like silver or gold or of other solid materials which do not break easily or deteriorate.

For the distribution of Communion, there are additional plates, dishes or metal cup-like containers. The latter is called a *ciborium*.

The *pall* is a square piece of cardboard enclosed in a white cloth container. The priest may place this upon the chalice to keep elements from dropping into the wine or Precious Blood.

*Cruets,* usually, but not necessarily of glass, contain the water and wine needed for the preparation of the gifts. Often, too, there is a larger glass vessel with the wine necessary for the many who will receive the Precious Blood; sometimes it is called a flagon.

During the Mass the priest washes his hands, saying quietly, "Lord, wash away my iniquity; cleanse me from my sin." The servers assist by bringing to the altar a *pitcher of water, basin,* and *hand towel.*

Some churches continue to ring a small *bell* just before the consecration at Mass as well as at the elevation of both the eucharistic bread and cup. This sound of the bell reminds people of the approaching solemn moment and adds festivity to the occasion.

We have examined the plan of the Mass, then studied both the vestments worn by the priest during the Eucharist and the materials used at the altar. In a way we call this serving with our head. Now we look at serving with our hands. Part II will answer the question: What does a server actually do during the Mass?

## Names to Know

*Deacon:* These men have received the sacrament of Holy Orders and the Church gives them the power and permission to preach the gospel, baptize, marry, and assist in a special way at Mass. Some are married; some are not. Some will move on to become priests; others remain permanently as deacons.

*Acolyte:* This is the technical title for altar servers. They may be younger or older, officially set aside for the position on a permanent basis or, more commonly, designated to serve for the immediate future on a temporary basis.

*Hospitality Minister:* More and more parishes have a group of men and women who greet people at the church entrances, welcome them to worship, and may hand to them the weekly bulletin and/or music aid. We call these volunteers hospitality ministers or, sometimes, simply greeters.

# — Part II—

# Serving with My Hands

**Julie, first year in college, nursing student, former server, office receptionist and weekend church sacristan.**

*Being an altar server has helped me grow both spiritually and personally. Spiritually it has allowed me to understand and appreciate God much more. As a college student, being away from home can be very lonely and stressful. More times than not, I have found myself turning towards God for comfort and guidance when no one else is there. Personally, altar serving has given me a chance to grow closer to others in the church community as well as participate in the Mass. I feel like I am giving a little of myself back to something that has given me so much.*

*When people ask me why I still am an altar server my answer to them is: I love being an altar server; it gives me a sense of belonging and peace.*

## ~ 4 ~

# At the Chair

**Tom, first year high school**

*When I am up on the altar I feel like I am not only serving the church but God as well. It makes me feel like I'm doing something good, something other people need me for.*

✠

**Sara, seventh grade, sister of Tom**

*When I'm altar serving, I feel closer to God. I get to help the younger kids who don't exactly know how to serve yet. I feel like I'm part of the Mass.*

✠

**Entrance Procession**

Weekend Masses usually begin with a procession from the entrance of the church to the sanctuary. It is part of the Introductory Rites, whose purpose is to form those present into a community, to prepare their hearts so they may properly hear God's word, and to help everyone celebrate the Eucharist worthily.

Generally two servers with candles lead the procession. There may also be another carrying the processional cross. And, on special occasions, a fourth altar server may head the procession swinging back and forth a censer with burning incense.

For example, on Passion or Palm Sunday, the Sacramentary describes the procession on that solemn occasion:

"If incense is used, the thurifer (server with incense) goes first with a lighted censer, followed by a cross bearer (with the cross suitably decorated) between two ministers with lighted candles, then the priest with the ministers. . . ."

Here are some practical suggestions for servers during the procession:

• Servers hold the outside hand on the upper part of the candle and the inside hand on the lower part.

• Those leading the procession move slightly slower than the ordinary pace for walking.

• When servers carry candles, cross or censer, they do not genuflect or bow before the altar or tabernacle even though the priest and others may do so. Bowing or genuflecting is awkward when carrying something. Moreover, servers bearing candles almost always spill melted wax when they bow or genuflect.

## At the Chair

At the end of the procession, the servers place the cross, candles, and perhaps censer in their proper places and move to either side of the presiding priest's chair. One of the servers needs to immediately pick up the Sacramentary and be ready to hold it for the priest. The priest may use this book of prayers to assist him with several parts of the Introductory Rites. However, he will almost certainly require the Sacramentary to read or sing the opening prayer.

When the prayer has been completed, the server returns the Sacramentary to its appointed place and then joins the priest and other servers at a chair beside the priest.

Here are some additional practical suggestions for the server at the chair during this beginning part of Mass:

• Hold the Sacramentary open to the proper page with both hands at the bottom of the book. Stand directly in front of the priest and maintain the book at the level he desires. Try to remain perfectly still while the priest proclaims this prayer.

• Follow the lead of the presiding priest during this part of Mass: when he sits, sit; when he stands, stand.

• While seated, keep both feet on the ground with both hands on your lap.

**The Sacramentary**

As servers gain experience, it would be helpful for them to learn in some detail the overall content of the Sacramentary.

The Sacramentary contains over two thousand prayers which the priest reads or sings—first from the chair, then at the altar and, finally, again from the chair.

We use the first four major sections of this book for Sundays and other solemn feasts.

1. *The Proper of the Seasons*. This section contains prayers for the Sundays and major celebrations of Advent, Christmas, Lent, Holy Week, Easter, and the Ordinary time of the year. The last season covers 34 Sundays, celebrated with green vestments, first between Christmas and Lent and then between Pentecost and Advent.

For each Sunday or feast there are three prayers: Opening Prayer (from the chair), Prayer over the Gifts (at the altar), and Prayer after Communion (from the chair).

2. *Order of Mass*. This section includes the regulations or rubrics for Mass and the standard prayers repeated by the priest at every Eucharist. It also contains 84 prefaces and numerous eucharistic prayers plus a series of solemn blessings and prayers over the people.

3. *The Proper of Saints*. This section presents the celebrations for saints throughout the calendar year from January through December. These observances vary in rank. For example, the celebration honoring St. Lawrence, Deacon and Martyr on August 10 ranks as a feast; the day recognizing St. Clare has a lesser rank, that of a memorial.

Sometimes, especially with the major feasts, the Proper of the Saints provides all three Mass prayers; on other occasions of lesser dignity, this section includes merely a proper Opening Prayer.

In those cases where only the Opening Prayer is given, the priest turns to this next part for the other prayers.

4. *Commons.* This section contains Mass prayers for the Dedication of a Church. It then provides what the book terms the Commons (Opening Prayer, Prayer over the Gifts and Prayer after Communion) for celebrations of the Blessed Virgin Mary, Martyrs, Pastors, Church Doctors, Virgins, and Holy Men or Women. The priest will use this section mainly in connection with the Proper of the Saints and mostly on weekdays.

The Sacramentary also provides a great number of prayers for many other situations like funerals and weddings. However, in a small book like this, it is not possible to describe these additional prayers in detail.

Here are some practical suggestions for the server in connection with the Sacramentary.

• On Sundays (and Saturday evenings), the priest ordinarily will use two of the several colored ribbons available to indicate the proper page for the celebration. One locates the prayers for the Prayer of the Season; the other locates the preface for this particular Mass.

• The priest may also choose additional ribbons to locate particular prayers in the Order of Mass.

• At the end of the Introductory Rites and after Communion, the server opens the Sacramentary to the ribbon indicating the correct page in the Proper of the Seasons.

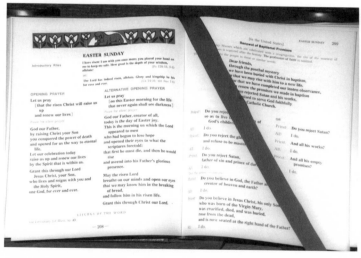

## The Recessional

Following the Prayer after Communion, the announcements, the blessing, and the dismissal, the priest and servers make a reverence to the altar. They then ordinarily exit from the sanctuary much as they entered it.

Here are some practical suggestions for the server about the recessional:

• After the servers gather cross and candles, they move to a designated spot on the floor and face the altar.

• The priest and other ministers make a profound bow to the altar, but the servers carrying cross and candles do not.

• The servers turn and lead the recession out of the church just as they led the procession into the sanctuary.

The servers have a relatively minor, but still significant role, in connection with the ambo and the biblical readings. We will discuss that task in the next chapter.

# By the Ambo

## Alan, eighth grade

*I enjoy being an altar server because it makes me feel closer to God. Also, I feel like I am making a contribution to the church, and serving helps me to meet new people. It is a good way to get involved with the church and the community.*

✠

## Lizzy, sixth grade, sister of Alan

*I like being an altar server because you get to help the priest and I like helping out.*

✠

What the Church now officially terms the ambo, as mentioned earlier, we formerly called the pulpit or lectern.

From that location in the sanctuary, the lector or reader proclaims readings assigned for that day. It is from there also that a priest or deacon shares the gospel passage and preaches the homily.

## Christ the Light

Jesus Christ declared himself to be the light of the world and a light shining in darkness. The Church also reminds us that Jesus is truly present when the scriptures are proclaimed during Mass. The bishops stated at the Second Vatican Council in 1963: Christ "is present in his word since it is he himself who speaks when the holy scriptures are read in the church" (Constitution on the Sacred Liturgy, no. 7).

To emphasize that presence and light, servers often hold the processional candles on either side of the ambo during the reading of the gospel.

Here are some practical suggestions connected with the gospel reading:

• The priest or deacon usually proclaims the gospel from a separate book. This Book of the Gospels is carried in the entrance procession and placed at the center of the altar.

• The priest or deacon, accompanied by the servers, picks up the book and in a brief, but solemn procession, takes it to the ambo.

• The servers face one another on either side of the ambo during the proclamation of the gospel.

## The Lectionary

The Book of Gospels contains the gospel texts taken from the Lectionary.

The Lectionary is not a Bible, but, instead, a book of biblical readings arranged for Masses over a three-year period. Persons who participate in the Eucharist every day during those three years will not hear every word printed in the Bible. But they will be exposed to much of both the Old and New Testament.

These scriptural readings have been arranged in a complex, but carefully thought out system.

Readings for Sundays and solemn feasts follow a three-year cycle (Readings A, B or C). Readings for weekdays observe a two-year cycle (Readings Year I or II).

The Lectionary follows a similar pattern to the Sacramentary.

*The Proper of the Seasons* contains two sections:

The first portion includes Sunday Readings for Advent, Christmas, Lent, the Easter Triduum and Season, the Seasons of the Year, and Solemnities of the Lord during the year.

The second portion includes Weekday Readings for Advent, Christmas, Lent, Easter, and the Seasons of the Year.

*The Proper of the Saints* contains readings for the saints according to their assigned dates in the calendar year.

The last part of the Lectionary includes a rich collection of readings for a great variety of celebrations including such occasions as marriages, funerals, Masses for the sick, and Thanksgiving Day.

## Love for Sacred Scripture

The Church loves the Bible.

The revised Lectionary first published over thirty years ago opens up more widely the sacred scriptures to those at Mass. Week after week and day after day those participating in the Eucharist hear a far greater selection of biblical passages than in previous years.

The Church hopes that through this Lectionary Catholics will develop a warm and living love for the Bible.

To emphasize the respect and reverence we have for the scriptural passages, the Church adds, in addition to the candles on either side of the ambo, several other gestures:

The people stand to honor Christ's presence in the gospel.

The priest or deacon makes the sign of the cross on the book and then on his forehead, lips and heart. The people in the congregation follow his example. By doing this we are saying in effect, "May I understand these words with my mind, speak them with my lips, and believe them in my heart."

After finishing his proclamation, the priest or deacon says, "The Gospel of the Lord." The people respond: "Praise to you, Lord Jesus Christ."

At the end of the reading, the priest or deacon kisses the open page as a sign of reverence for the holy word.

During some solemn occasions, the priest or deacon also incenses the gospel book.

## Incense

When the Mass celebration includes incense, the priest or deacon usually incenses the Book of Gospels at the ambo. He does this by a single swing of the *censer* center, left and right.

Here are some practical suggestions for the server in connection with the incensation at the ambo.

• The server takes the censer and vessel of incense or boat to the priest at the chair and opens the censer. The priest scoops a bit of incense and sprinkles it upon the burning charcoal.

• After a priest or deacon proclaims the introductory greeting for the gospel, the server hands him the censer. When the censer is returned to her/him, the server steps back a few feet and remains there during the proclamation of the gospel.

## Word and Sacrament

The cloud of sweet-smelling incense directed toward the Book of Gospels symbolizes our respect for God's word. It also is a sign of the power this biblical text has to lift up our minds and hearts to God.

As we saw in the Plan of the Mass, there are two mountain-like movements in the Eucharist. We first speak to God and God speaks to us; we give to God and God gives to us.

The gospel, homily, creed, and prayer of the faithful concludes the first mountain which centered around the ambo and God's word. Now we move to the altar for the second mountain or the Liturgy of the Eucharist.

Some churches, to indicate this shift, have servers move candles from the ambo to the altar or, at this time, light the candles near the altar.

However, the two mountains are closely connected. God is present and speaks to us in the Liturgy of the Word. God is also present in a unique manner during the Liturgy of the Eucharist and gives to us Christ himself at Communion.

Moreover, the spoken word prepares us for the eucharistic food to come. It also points to the re-creation or re-enactment of the Last Supper about to take place.

Our final treatment of "Serving with My Hands" will examine the functions of servers near the altar during this Liturgy of the Eucharist.

## ~ 6 ~

# Near the Altar

### Nate, third year high school

*I like being an altar server because not only am I helping out great priests but I am also serving God. The priests need someone to help them and in 4th grade when Father Champlin asked me to serve I was encouraged by my parents and thought it would be a good experience.*

### Michael, first year high school

*When I started out serving with my brother I was afraid of making a mistake in front of all the people in church. I knew it was a good thing to do but I didn't want to do it. Even when I started serving I didn't really enjoy altar serving as much as I do now. Now I look forward to filling in for someone who is absent. I guess it took a while to feel comfortable on the altar.*

In every church there is ordinarily an altar fastened and fixed to the floor in a permanent way. It also should be located within the sanctuary in such fashion that the attention of the congregation naturally focuses upon the altar. The stability and the centrality of the altar show that it represents Christ Jesus the Living Stone.

The Bible reminds us of this last truth, the link between Jesus and stone. Scripture urges us to come to Christ, "a living stone, rejected by human beings but chosen and precious in God's sight" (1 Peter 2:4).

It is upon the altar that several sacred events occur: the sacrifice of the cross is made present under sacramental signs; people gather at this table of the Lord to share in Communion; all present join in giving thanks to God which is the meaning of the Eucharist and what it does.

The altar should be free-standing, making it possible for the ministers to walk around it easily. The altar also needs to be so designed that Mass can be celebrated facing the people whenever possible.

The altar ideally should be of natural stone because of the meaning we mentioned above, although other solid, attractive and well made materials may be used.

Relics of saints are often placed within the altar itself.

Churches built in recent years usually have only one altar as a sign of unity, indicating that there is only one Christ and one Eucharist.

We place at least one white cloth on the altar when Mass is celebrated to remind all that Christ was wrapped in a cloth and then placed in his tomb. It also recalls to us that Jesus gives his Body and Blood in the banquet of Communion.

Candles placed either on or around the altar add a sense of reverence and festivity to the celebration.

A cross with the figure of Christ crucified upon it stands on or near the altar to remind us of Jesus' saving passion for others.

We place on the altar only those items needed at the time: the Book of the Gospels from the beginning until the proclamation of the Gospel; the chalice, paten, corporal, purificator, and sacramentary from the presentation of the gifts until the end.

Flowers, placed around, but not on the altar, add to the beauty of the celebration. However, there should be fewer flowers during Advent and none at all during Lent.

**Preparing the Altar**

Following completion of the General Intercessions or Prayer of the Faithful, all sit while ushers take up the collection. In the meantime, servers normally prepare the altar, although members of the congregation may do so.

The altar cloth usually remains on the altar throughout the entire Mass. The servers, therefore, need only to bring to the altar the corporal, purificator, sacramentary, chalice, and paten or plate with the large host upon it. In some parishes, candles from the ambo are moved to a place near the altar or the candles located next to the altar are lighted.

Many churches on weekends have a solemn procession of servers and a few people from the congregation bringing the gifts needed for the Liturgy of the Eucharist from the entrance of the church to the priest at the altar. These would include the hosts, the wine, and perhaps the small cruet or jar of water. Receptacles of money offerings may also be brought forward, received by the priest or deacon and placed on the sanctuary floor in front of the altar.

Here are some practical suggestions for the servers in connection with preparing the altar:

• Two servers with candles may leave the sanctuary and move to the church entrance. There they meet the gift bearers, turn and lead them to the altar. At the steps they part and wait until the priest and/or deacon has received the offerings before returning the candles to their places.

• The corporal is unfolded and laid in the center of the altar near the edge. The paten is placed upon the corporal and the chalice with the purificator off the corporal and to the right.

• A server leaves the Sacramentary open to the desired ribbon and either at an angle to the left of the corporal or at the center off the corporal according to the preference of the presiding priest.

## Water, Incense and Washing

The priest at one point during the preparation and "blessing" ceremony, takes the water cruet from the server and pours a drop or two into the vessel containing the wine.

That simple gesture symbolizes some significant teachings of the Catholic Christian faith. As the drops of water disappear into the wine, we recall the blend of the divine and human natures in Jesus and the divine grace which we human beings receive through the sacrament of baptism.

As he carefully pours the few drops of water into the wine, the priest or deacon says quietly: "Through the mystery of this water and wine may we come to share in the divinity of Christ who humbled himself to share in our humanity."

The priest may also *incense* the altar. He incenses the gifts at the center of the altar and then walks around the altar swinging the censer. Afterwards the server or deacon may incense the priest and the congregation.

With the gifts prepared and the altar incensed, the priest *washes his hands,* saying quietly: "Lord wash away my iniquity, cleanse me from my sin."

In the early Christian days at Mass, people actually brought to the altar items like food and animals needed for the priest's support and for the poor. Washing of the priest's hands was, consequently, a real necessity at that time. This no longer is generally the case. Instead the Church views the washing gesture as a symbol that our hearts need cleansing before we move on to the sacred action of the Eucharist.

Here are some suggestions for servers in connection with these three actions:

• One server takes the water cruet from the table to the altar, presents it to the priest or deacon and, when he hands the cruet back, returns it to the table.

• After bread and wine are prepared, one or two servers bring censer and boat to the priest or deacon, if it will be used. They then stand away from the altar during the incensation. Afterwards they return both items to their places.

• Two servers bring a pitcher, basin, and a special large towel for the washing of hands. Since this is intended to be a real washing, the server should not hesitate to pour an ample amount of water over the priest's hands.

## Bells

Ringing a small bell or bells several times during Mass was standard procedure years ago. That practice has disappeared in many parishes, although it is still permitted. Where a particular church does retain this action, the bell or bells are rung before the consecration, often when the priest extends his hands over the gifts. They may also be rung at the elevation of the consecrated host and wine.

**Clearing of Altar**

During or after the distribution of Communion, servers remove the various vessels from the altar and return them to the table by the side. In some churches the server brings water to the priest who cleanses the chalice at the altar.

The server takes the Sacramentary to the chair for use there with the Prayers after Communion, announcements, and possible additional blessings.

We have now completed our study of serving with my hands, looking at what servers actually do during Mass at the chair, by the ambo, and near the altar. In our final section, Part III, we will discuss serving with our heart or the inner spirit with which we carry out these actions.

# — Part III—

# Serving with My Heart

**Frank, 53, father of three children under ten, a life-long financial investment advisor and an occasional server at Immaculate Conception Cathedral's weekday noon Mass.**

*When we admire a great athlete or musician, then getting near to that person seems to give us joy. If that person asks us to carry his or her gym bag or instrument, we would do it gladly, feeling that it is an honor rather than a chore. After being of help, we might feel something special has rubbed off on us. One might call it a "high." I believe that on the altar (God's banquet table) through the words of the consecration, Jesus is made present. In this simple place, our King humbly comes to be with all of us, his friends.*

*As a server, the spiritual joy of being close to our King and assisting his chosen priest cannot be matched on earth. Like Mary*

69

*who, in awe, received her Savior into her womb and then visited Elizabeth, carrying to her the message of God's presence, so I feel that my service is another way of showing my love for the good Lord who saved me. Serving is an action that fills a need to get closer to God, but it is also an expression of my joy when my desire to be available to God is being fulfilled.*

# ~ 7 ~

# **Believing in the Mass**

### Severin, Fourth Grade

*I feel helpful to God and everyone else, because I am helping everyone to get ready in Mass. And it feels better to be helping than to be watching what I could do as an altar server.*

✠

### Peter, older brother of Severin and Second Year High School

*I like being an altar server because it makes me feel like I am a part of the Mass. It keeps me busy. When I am in the pew watching Mass, I feel a little bored, but when I am on the altar I am busy with different jobs. I feel that being an altar server is a privilege because when you are up on the altar you feel good inside.*

When Jesus was about 30 he began his public life of preaching and teaching. Early on during that period, he once told his close followers to get into a boat and make their way across a body of water to its other side. This was Lake Gennesaret, or better known to us as the Sea of Galilee.

After they left, he sent away the crowd listening to him speak and went off by himself up on a mountain to pray. He remained there alone throughout the evening praying to his Father in heaven.

His followers meanwhile had made their way a few miles out into the water. However, this is a dangerous lake or sea. When the wind becomes strong or a storm arrives, and storms do arise quite suddenly, its waters become very rough and the waves, high and unruly.

Jesus' followers ran into one of those storms.

The fierce wind and huge waves were tossing the boat around like it was a toy. Water began to fill the little vessel and his followers, despite their frantic efforts, thought they were sinking.

It was between 3 and 6 a.m., the middle of the night. Frightened as they were, these friends of Jesus suddenly saw him coming toward them walking on the sea. The sight of Christ moving over the water terrified them even more. Overcome with fear, they cried out, "It is a ghost!"

Jesus immediately reassured them by saying: "Take heart, it is I; do not be afraid."

Peter, the leader of these followers, then made this request of Christ: "Lord, if it is you, command me to come to you on the water."

Jesus replied, "Come," and motioned to Peter to make his way toward him.

Peter got out of the boat and started walking on the water in Jesus' direction.

However, when Peter saw just how strong the wind was and how high the waves, he became frightened again and, beginning to sink, shouted, "Lord, save me!"

Jesus immediately stretched out his hand and caught Peter. He then scolded him: "You of little faith, why did you doubt?"

Christ and Peter then walked together back to the boat. When they got into it, the wind died down and the sea became calm.

Everyone in the boat then bowed down before Jesus and with faith said: "Truly you are the Son of God" (Matthew 14:22-33).

## Faith

It is almost impossible to define very precisely certain major things in the world around us. Life and love, for example, or birth and death. Faith is one of these matters or realities which defy a definition. Instead we try to describe it.

Our now retired Bishop of Syracuse, Frank Harrison, described faith in this way: It is a power or quality within which makes it possible for us to look beyond and discover something more. We go beyond what is before us and discover there the presence of God.

This should become clearer through the following examples:

We look beyond beauty and discover the wonderful God behind the beauty.

Sometime soon, gaze for several minutes at a spectacular sunset or a star in the sky, at a colorful flower or a sturdy tree. Then imagine God the Creator behind these beautiful creations.

We look beyond burdens and discover a caring God present in the midst of those troubles.

My great niece walked away unharmed from a terrible car pileup on a California freeway. She searched for three years seeking an answer to her questions: Why was I spared and others not?

Finally, her painful search brought her to faith in God, a caring God who is close to the broken hearted and saves those who are crushed in spirit. This loving God brought something good out of that bad accident (Psalm 34:19).

We look beyond blessings and discover the God above who is the giver of every good gift.

Some things we work for and apparently earn ourselves. But many other blessings just come to us. With faith we can go beyond these kinds of gifts and recognize the gracious God who constantly showers blessings upon us.

We look beyond elements of the Mass and discover the Risen Jesus present in and through them.

We glance at all the people gathered in church for Mass and recognize that the Lord is dwelling among us. He said: "For where two or three are gathered in my name, I am there among them" (Matthew 18:20).

We hear words from the Bible and believe that God is speaking to us.

We look at the consecrated host and chalice of consecrated wine raised slightly above the altar or we receive the Body and Blood of Christ in Communion. With faith we move beyond these experiences to discover the Risen Jesus present there in a special way.

## Practical Consequences

Here are a few practical consequences of faith for an altar server:

• At Mass only the priest can transform the hosts from ordinary bread into the holy Body of Christ. Unconsecrated breads require his action before they become the consecrated hosts for distribution at Communion.

• Similarly, only the priest can transform the wine into the Precious Blood of Christ. The unconsecrated wine likewise requires his action before it becomes the consecrated element for distribution at Holy Communion.

• Faith in the Risen Christ's Presence is the reason why altar servers hold candles by the ambo during the gospel, kneel next to the altar for the eucharistic prayer, and make a reverence (bow or genuflection) whenever they pass by the tabernacle.

Prayer keeps our faith alive and strengthens it. We will now discuss finding time for prayer.

## ~ 8 ~

# Being a Person of Prayer

Peter, first year high school, also a lector, weekend sacristan, brother of Laura (Introduction) and Rachel (Chapter 3).

### What Being a Server Means to Me

*When I was in 4th grade, my sister Laura and I began altar serving. We both wanted to serve all the time, and every week we'd hope we could serve. But eventually, I honestly began to dread altar serving. I'd go to church and hope no one would ask me to go and help. For a while, I didn't want to serve.*

*Then one day it hit me. This is what the Mass is all about. There is no greater honor than to stand on the altar helping the priest prepare the body and blood of Christ.*

*Today, I love being an altar server. Whenever there aren't enough servers, I gladly help. I am glad that I've found the meaning I had once lost in this wonderful duty. Being an altar server puts you one step above the rest of the congregation. Instead of just "going to" Mass, you're actually a part of it. It is a sacred responsibility that I enjoy and would honestly feel much less fulfilled if I were to not be a part of it. Being an altar server is a great thing.*

✛

At the time of Jesus leprosy was a terrible affliction. Doctors today call it Hansen's Disease and new drugs can curb some of the symptoms. But during Christ's days, not only did the disease destroy one's body, but most persons also considered it highly contagious. Moreover, in the land where Jesus taught, the main religion judged lepers also to be spiritually unclean.

For all these reasons, people avoided individuals burdened with leprosy. In addition, the law demanded that lepers carry a little bell and when anyone drew near them they were to ring it and shout, "Unclean, unclean."

One day Jesus was preaching in a town where a man full of leprosy lived. We can imagine how ugly he looked and how the leper frightened all those who had gathered to hear Christ speak.

Part of his fingers, ears, and toes would have rotted away and his face covered with sores because of the disease. The crowd probably shuddered at the sight and drew away from him lest they become infected with the dreaded illness.

The leper, however, saw Jesus and went right up to him. He fell down before Christ and pleaded with him, saying: "Lord, if you choose, you can make me clean."

Unlike the fearful and withdrawing crowd, Jesus stretched out his hand and touched him.

Christ then said: "I do choose. Be made clean."

The Bible tells us that "Immediately the leprosy left him" (Luke 5:12-13).

News about this miraculous healing quickly spread throughout the area. Great crowds began to gather around Christ and listen to him speak. They also hoped that he would cure them of their own ailments and diseases.

Jesus did continue to teach and heal them, but after this hard work he withdrew from the crowd, went off to a deserted place and prayed.

The Bible also tells us that one evening Christ went up on a mountain to spend the night in prayer to God (Luke 5:16, 6:12). When daylight arrived, Jesus came down the mountain, chose his twelve apostles and continued to cure all who came to him.

**A Time to Pray and a Time to Work**

Notice the pattern in the life of Jesus. He worked hard at teaching and healing, but regularly went off by himself for some time to pray. He also prayed before making any major decision and resuming his work of helping others.

Everyone who has ever walked in Christ's footsteps by trying to do good for others has also followed his example. They, like Jesus, have found time to pray each day before and after their work.

• Centuries ago St. Francis was constantly teaching and giving advice. But he frequently returned to Assisi, made his way to an isolated wooded area, and there prayed by himself for perhaps a month.

• The late Cardinal Bernardin of Chicago, during the last twenty years of his life, arose early every morning and spent an hour in prayer. Before he began his work of responding to phone calls and meeting with many people, this cardinal set aside the first part of each day for speaking and listening to God.

• Mother Teresa's Missionaries of Charity serve the poorest of the poor throughout the world. These sisters, too, pray for a long period of time prior to leaving their convent for this noble work and upon returning to the convent.

## Practical Consequences

What we have inside us comes across to others. People can tell if we love others, believe in God, or pray often. Moreover, persons in church expect altar servers to have those inner qualities of love, faith, and prayer. These attitudes will influence the way servers carry candles, hold their hands, or stand by the altar.

Finding a few minutes each day to be by ourselves and to be with God helps keep alive those inner qualities and makes them stronger. These moments are not only for reciting prayers, but also for speaking personally with Jesus. We can visit with him as a friend visits with a friend, often talking about other friends in need.

There are quiet times within Mass which give us moments to pray very personally. For example, when the priest says or sings "Let us pray," after each reading or the homily, throughout the eucharistic prayer, and during the precious moments after Communion. Servers who believe and pray will take good advantage of those quiet moments. Members of the congregation will notice that.

As a server, we want to do everything right and may worry too much about that. God wishes us to take our serving seriously, but not to fret over our tasks. The next and last chapter in this book will offer some suggestions about how to balance both goals: getting things right and yet not over-worrying.

# Acting in a Reverent, but Relaxed Way

"Del," eighty plus years old, worked at a variety of jobs during her active decades. Each day she comes to the Cathedral for the 12:10 p.m. Mass. She assists there as an altar server and eucharistic minister. Her response to my inquiry about the joy she experiences through serving came in two forms.

First, Del enclosed in her letter a leaflet which she has obviously carried for years in a well-worn prayer book. Entitled *The Infinite Value of the Holy Mass*, it begins with these statements:

*The Holy Mass is the highest form of worship. It is the sacrifice of Calvary renewed. One Mass gives God more praise and thanksgiving, makes more atonement for sin and pleads more eloquently than does the combined and eternal worship of all the souls in heaven, on earth and in Purgatory.*

Second, she sent along a commercial "Thank You" card. Pasted on the inside left page was this clipping from an unnamed source:

*At Mass, we remember the love of God who created us, Jesus who saves us, and the Holy Spirit who sets us free. We also call to mind our family, friends, fellow believers, and the entire communion of saints in this wonderful act of Christian unity—the Mass.*

On the inside right page of that card, Del had written "Dear Father" just above the printed text which read:

*This note brings friendly wishes*
*And appreciation, too*
*Because you are so thoughtful*
*And I want to say "Thank you!"*

Del then added her personal greeting:

*[Thank you] for allowing me to serve at this most wonderful act of Christian unity. It's like a bridge between Heaven and earth. We take time to speak to Our Father. There are many blessings for the living and dead. We feed our soul and are blessed before we leave. May we always love the Mass—our best help for now and eternity.*

*Your friend*
*"Del"*

## Loaves and Fishes

Jesus' reputation as a powerful preacher and remarkable healer quickly spread around the Holy Land. People, consequently, came in great numbers to hear him speak and to see him heal. However, the crowds were so large and demanding that Christ and his apostles had very little time to eat or sleep.

To give themselves a needed break, Jesus and his friends got into a boat and went across the lake to a deserted place on the other side. However, the crowd saw where they were going and raced along the shore to that spot, arriving there before the boat did.

Despite being very tired and hungry, Jesus felt sorry for the huge number of people and once again began to teach them about many things.

He continued for hours, but as the sun started to set, the apostles said to their Master: "It is very late. We are hungry and so are these people. There are no stores or restaurants or homes around here. Tell this crowd to go to the nearest towns and villages and buy food for themselves."

Jesus instead bluntly commanded: "Give them something to eat yourselves."

The puzzled apostles responded: "There are about 5,000 people here and we have only a little cash in our pockets, just a few coins. How are we going to buy enough bread for so many?"

Christ replied, "How many loaves of bread do you have with you right now? Go and find out."

They returned shortly thereafter and answered: "Five loaves and two fish."

Jesus then told the apostles to have this huge gathering sit down on the green grass in groups of a hundred or fifty.

After they were settled in place, Christ, taking the loaves and fish, looked up to heaven. He first blessed and broke the loaves of bread. Next he shared them with his followers, ordering them to set these pieces before the large crowd. Finally, he divided the fish among everyone present.

What happened subsequently was remarkable, a miracle, a deed unable to be explained. Everyone ate and felt full afterwards. Moreover, after all had eaten, Jesus' close followers found some wicker baskets and began to gather up the scattered bread pieces and untouched fish. They filled twelve baskets with what remained. Five loaves and two fish; 5,000 fed; twelve baskets of leftovers. Unbelievable!

## A Major Event

There are, of course, four gospels inspired by God which present to us the life and teachings of Jesus. This marvelous multiplication of the loaves and fishes is the only miracle which appears in all four. Servers should find it interesting and valuable to read these four parallel or, in other words, similar, but slightly different accounts: Matthew 14:13-21; Mark 6:32-44; Luke 9:10-17; John 6:1-13.

Since Jesus performed many miraculous deeds, why would this event be given such special attention? There are several possible explanations.

• It anticipated what Christ did and does for us with the Eucharist. At the Last Supper and at Mass he changes the bread and wine into his own Body and Blood so that many, even countless people can eat and drink this spiritual food.

• It reflects Jesus' prediction about a banquet later in heaven (Matthew 8:11; 26:29).

• It recalls how God fed the hungry and grumbling chosen people of Israel in the desert with a unique bread from heaven (Exodus 16).

• It may also refer to the time in the Old Testament when the prophet Elisha fed one hundred men with twenty barley loaves. There, too, God through his prophet promised that all would have enough to eat and there would still be some left over (2 Kings 4:42-44).

**Awesome**

When Moses was caring for his father-in-law's flock, he came to Horeb, the mountain of God. There this man who was to lead his people to the promised land saw a bush burning, but without burning up. Moses thought to himself: "I must go over to look at this remarkable sight."

When he drew closer, God called out to him from the bush: "Do not come any nearer. Take off your sandals for you are standing on holy ground."

Moses did as commanded and also hid his face in his hands for he was afraid to look at God (Exodus 3:1-6).

Moses was awestruck. He stood in awe before God.

Those who witnessed Jesus' mighty deeds during his life on earth often reacted similarly.

For example, when Christ stilled the wind and calmed the sea during a violent storm, his friends in the boat which moments earlier was sinking were filled with awe and amazement. Who is this man, they said, who commands the wind and the sea and they obey him? (Luke 8:22-25).

Members of several major religions today respond in the same way before our awesome God.

In the Jewish tradition, faithful members strictly observe the Sabbath as a day of rest and worship; men wear a skull cap called a yarmulke (the orthodox all the time, the conservatives while at prayer); bowing before God is a frequent gesture.

In the Muslim tradition, believers kneel down on the ground and bend with forehead touching the earth five times each day as they worship the one holy God.

In the Catholic tradition, we sign ourselves with holy water when entering a church, speak there in softer tones, and bow or genuflect during Mass.

Believers, therefore, act with reverence when in the presence of God.

## Down-to-Earth

While Jesus performed awesome miracles that only God can do, Christ also walked among us in a very human way.

He was born in a cave stable because there was no room at the inn.

He grew angry when some people took advantage of others.

He changed water into wine at a wedding feast.

He felt hungry and tired at times.

He ate with sinners and welcomed them.

He wept when a friend had died.

He told his followers to gather up the leftover loaves lest anything would go to waste.

He gave us the Holy Eucharist as a sacred meal in which there would be crumbs on the table and during which wine might occasionally be spilled.

He knew sorrow and fear before he died.

He said "I thirst" while on the cross.

He also knows that his followers today, including servers, are also human, willing but weak, and do make mistakes.

## Practical Connections for Servers

• When preparing for Mass, think of Moses before the burning bush or the apostles after Jesus stilled the storm and strive to have that same sense of awe and wonder.

• Perform all actions during Mass with great reverence, aware that you are in the presence of the awesome God.

• Be relaxed and natural, knowing that you are not perfect, mistakes will happen and Jesus understands.

God wants many boys and girls, men and women to experience the great joy of being an altar server. We hope that this book will help many achieve that goal.

# Appendix

## Blessing of Servers

*The Book of Blessings* approved for use in the United States contains an "Order for the Blessing of Altar Servers, Sacristans, Musicians and Others" (Chapter 62, Numbers 1847-1870, pages 783-793).

It provides a service during Mass or in a celebration of the Word of God.

Normally the pastor gives the blessing, but he may delegate another priest or deacon to do so.

## Prayers for Altar Servers

This petition, adapted from the Order for the Blessing of Altar Servers, might be used occasionally on weekends in the General Intercessions or Prayer of the Faithful.

"For our altar servers, that the light of Christ may shine in their hearts, we pray to the Lord."

**Prayer before Serving**

The presiding priest, deacon, or other leader of worship might recite these prayers (also adapted from the Order for the Blessing of Servers) with the servers and other liturgical ministers prior to Mass or to the particular service.

*God of glory,*
*your beloved Son has shown us*
*that true worship comes from humble and con-*
   *trite hearts.*
*Bless our brothers and sisters,*
*who have responded to the needs of our parish*
*and wish to commit themselves to your service*
   *as altar servers and liturgical ministers.*
*Grant that their ministries may be fruitful*
*and our worship pleasing in your sight.*
*We ask this through Christ our Lord.*

*Lord God,*
*you give to each person*
*the gift of your Spirit for the building up of the*
   *Church.*
*Bless us and keep us all in your love.*
*We ask this through Christ our Lord.*

# Index